To my mother, Sally, who loved all plants,
including weeds but especially roses – C.G.

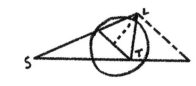

To my best friend, Mikołaj – G.H.

**Q** | **The Quarto Group**

Inspiring | Educating | Creating | Entertaining

Brimming with creative inspiration, how-to
projects and useful information to enrich your
everyday life, Quarto is a favourite destination for
those pursuing their interests and passions.

First Published in 2022 by Wide Eyed Editions, an imprint of The Quarto Group.
The Old Brewery, 6 Blundell Street, London N7 9BH, United Kingdom.
T (0)20 7700 6700  F (0)20 7700 8066  www.Quarto.com

A catalogue record for this book is available from the British Library.

ISBN 978-0-7112-7006-0

The illustrations were created digitally.
Set in Caffeine, Pacifico and Museo.

Published by Georgia Amson-Bradshaw
Designed by Myrto Dimitrakoulia
Commissioned by Lucy Brownridge
Edited by Hattie Grylls
Production by Dawn Cameron

Manufactured in Guangdong, China TT 052022

9 8 7 6 5 4 3 2 1

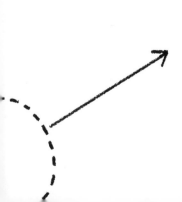

# Clive Gifford • Gosia Herba

# POWERED by PLANTS

## MEET THE TREES, FLOWERS AND VEGETATION THAT INSPIRE OUR EVERYDAY TECHNOLOGY

WIDE EYED EDITIONS

# CONTENTS

# DEAR READER,

Did you know that researchers are making new crash helmets stronger and safer thanks to a fruit called the pomelo? Or that humble coconuts are inspiring research into earthquake-proof buildings? What about willow trees, which have led to millions of people getting relief from headaches and other pains?

In this book, you will meet some of the most amazing celebrity super-plants that power our world. You'll see just how us plants are motivating people to invent and engineer amazing new solutions to difficult problems – from how to keep crops pest-free to how to produce fuels and materials that don't pollute the atmosphere.

After all, when it comes to working with nature, we're the experts. We've been flourishing in harmony for millions of years. We recycle nutrients and nurture soils and provide homes and food for billions of creatures, big and small. We've developed amazing shapes, surfaces and ways of coping with our environment and now, people are flocking to us for help.

Discover some of the genius ways in which people are copying our tried-and-tested methods to tackle disease-carrying mosquitoes, make eco-friendly plastics or produce super-slippery ships that use less fuel.

You'll never look at flowers, trees or seaweed in the same way again!

Yours sincerely,

*Tumbleweed*

# ··· Bamboo ···
# MIRACLE MATERIAL

I'm the fastest growing plant on the planet. Well, my species is (there are over 1,000 of us). I can grow up to 90 centimetres in a single day – beat that, other plants! My siblings all grow pretty fast as well and we are found in dense thickets across Asia. People find our young shoots tasty, but not as much as giant pandas; they eat up to 35 kilograms of bamboo a day. Greedy!

My hollow woody stems are light but strong. Engineers say I have great tensile strength – that means I'm very bendy. Humans have made use of me as a flexible friend for thousands of years. They've bent me into bows, fishing poles and furniture and bundled me together to build bamboo houses, fences, and other structures. I'm still used in parts of Asia today to make light but strong scaffolding building sites for skyscrapers.

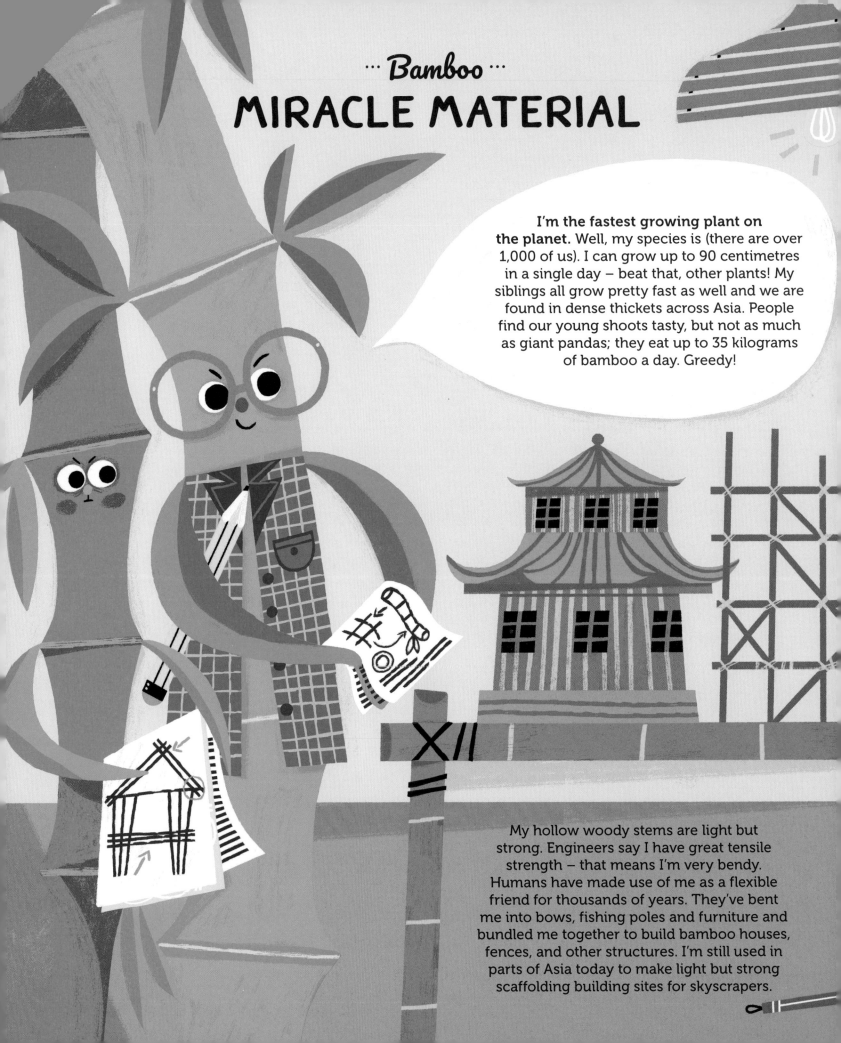

The ancient Chinese found more uses for me than any other civilisation. Before there was paper, they cut me into strips to form simple notebooks to write on. They also made flutes and other musical instruments from me. More than 1,000 years ago, my stems were filled with explosive black powder. When it was set alight, off I flew to become the first rockets and fireworks.

BAMBOO STALK → FIBRE → WOOL → FABRIC

Flute SYMPHONY

Gymnastics

FIREWORKS

Giant PANDA

ENCOUNTER with PANDA

KNITTING

YARN

YOGA

•house•

SCAFFOLDS•

HOW TO BUILD

A SKYSCRAPE

PANDA'S KITCHEN

I LOVE GRASS

In the past few years, scientists in China learned how to process hollow fibres from my stems to make a soft, breathable fabric. This fabric dries faster than cotton and is much greener than plastic fabrics like polyester and acrylic, which are made from oil. I also have less impact on the environment than cotton as I don't need lots of chemicals to grow and require only one-third of the water.

**I may reach up to 35 metres tall and look like a tree, but I'm actually the most useful grass on Earth!**

# ··· Vines ···
# TOUGH TWISTERS

Vines have been helping people build bridges and other constructions for thousands of years. We're a big group of hundreds of species of climbing plants that have long, flexible stems. You might know some of us, such as ivy, passion flowers, wisteria, sweet peas, clematis and grapevines. There are many, many more and we all have a head for heights!

As we grow upwards, we keep ourselves attached and anchored in many different ways. Some of us wind and wrap ourselves around a branch or other object for grip. This is called twining. Others, like the Virginia creeper, use sticky pads to fix themselves in place.

Ancient people found that by twisting a number of our strands together, they could make long coils of material that would support their weight and more. They tied these across ravines and above rivers to form simple suspension bridges. They used lots of our strands to attach wood or bundles of reeds together to form rafts and the hulls, or frames, of early boats. They also tied our long stems around giant rocks to haul them from place to place to build statues, temples and palaces.

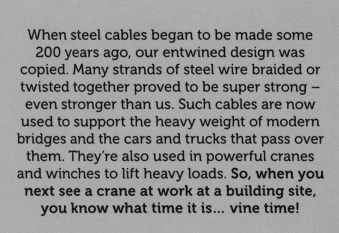

When steel cables began to be made some 200 years ago, our entwined design was copied. Many strands of steel wire braided or twisted together proved to be super strong – even stronger than us. Such cables are now used to support the heavy weight of modern bridges and the cars and trucks that pass over them. They're also used in powerful cranes and winches to lift heavy loads. **So, when you next see a crane at work at a building site, you know what time it is... vine time!**

··· Coconut palm ···

# EARTHQUAKE–PROOF PLANT

I'm the most famous tree in the tropics. My thick trunk is resistant to salt water, so it's used to make huts and boats. I'm topped by a graceful crown of giant leaves – some of which can grow more than 6 metres long. These are used to thatch roofs and walls, make bags and wrap food before cooking. In total, I can grow up to 30 metres high and live for 80 years.

However, my most famous feature is my rock-hard fruit, the coconut. I grow up to seventy-five of these a season. Beneath the outer layer is a very hairy husk. It's used to produce a tough fibre called coir, which can be turned into robust ropes, baskets, mats and brushes. If the husk is burned, it gives off a special smoke that repels mosquitoes. Is there no end to my fruit's usefulness?

Beneath all that hairy stuff is a hard wooden shell and inside that, lots of coconut water – good enough to drink. As the coconut ripens, the amount of water drops and a white fleshy pulp develops on the inside of the shell which is tasty and can be pressed to produce coconut oil.

OUTER COAT OF FRUIT

WHITE FLESH

COIR FIBRE

SHELL

COCONUT WATER

SEED COAT

COCONUT MILK

LADDER-LIKE PATTERN OF SHELL CELLS

The shell of my coconuts used to get next to no attention but now, scientists have found that they contain lots of cells in a ladder-shaped pattern. These seem to deflect the forces of an impact around the shell, preventing a crack going right through the shell and splitting the coconut open. If materials like my ladders could be embedded inside concrete to do a similar job, then more earthquake-proof buildings could be built. They could also help produce structures that don't crack and topple when the ground starts shaking. **It may sound unlikely, but if a brilliant solution already exists in nature, you'd be (coco) nuts not to use it!**

# ··· Giant water lily ···
# SUPER STRUCTURE

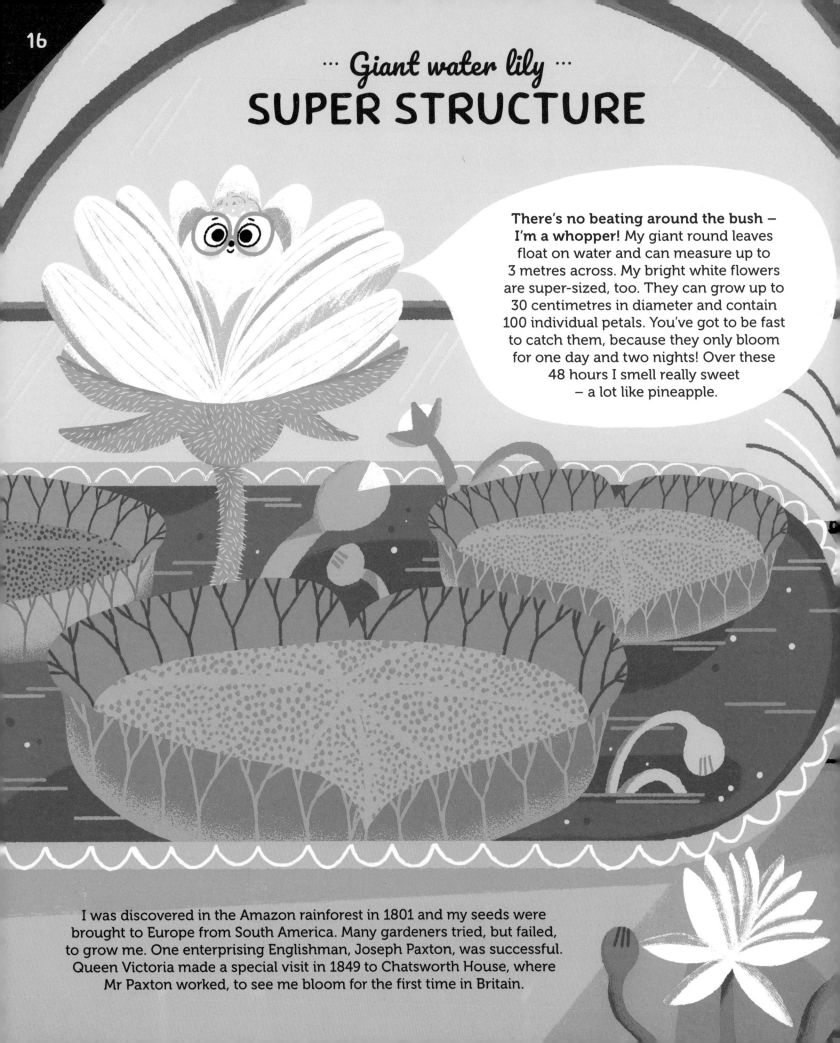

**There's no beating around the bush – I'm a whopper!** My giant round leaves float on water and can measure up to 3 metres across. My bright white flowers are super-sized, too. They can grow up to 30 centimetres in diameter and contain 100 individual petals. You've got to be fast to catch them, because they only bloom for one day and two nights! Over these 48 hours I smell really sweet – a lot like pineapple.

I was discovered in the Amazon rainforest in 1801 and my seeds were brought to Europe from South America. Many gardeners tried, but failed, to grow me. One enterprising Englishman, Joseph Paxton, was successful. Queen Victoria made a special visit in 1849 to Chatsworth House, where Mr Paxton worked, to see me bloom for the first time in Britain.

Mr Paxton proved not only a great gardener but a smart engineer. He based his design of a grand new exhibition hall on me and my amazing natural engineering. It beat 233 other architects' designs and was opened in 1851 as the Crystal Palace. The building was made of glass supported by ribs made of iron and stood longer than five football pitches. **It was a roaring success and inspired other buildings to be built following designs found in nature.**

• JOSEPH PAXTON •

• THE CRYSTAL PALACE •

Mr Paxton remained fascinated by my giant leaves. They are waxy on top but underneath, they are braced by sturdy ribs that spread out from my centre. Short mid-ribs run between each main rib, reinforcing the entire structure. As a result, my leaves possess great strength. This was demonstrated by Paxton's seven-year-old daughter, Annie, standing on me in the water. We were perfectly fine and didn't sink!

# ··· Pomelo ···
# CRASH-TEST CITRUS

I'm a tree from China and Southeast Asia but I now grow in lots of warm places. My trunk can twist, turn and support a canopy of evergreen leaves. My fruit is big in China but isn't as well known elsewhere. That's a shame as I think it's absolutely amazing. Let me tell you more about it and myself.

I produce the world's largest and heaviest citrus fruit, called the pomelo. It can grow to the size of a basketball and weigh almost 2 kilograms – beat that lemons, oranges and nectarines! Its peel is a greenish-yellow colour and, inside, the flesh is mild and sometimes sweet. Unlike grapefruit, it's very rarely bitter.

You'd expect that such a heavy fruit falling from my highest branches, up to 15 metres above the ground, would end in a splattered mess. You'd be wrong! My fruit has a secret shock-absorber inside. Below the waxy peel's surface is a thick network of cells and spaces between them. It's a bit like a sponge. The spaces get bigger, and are filled with juice and air, the deeper you go into the fruit. Thud! As it falls and hits the ground, the spaces in the fruit collapse to absorb the force of the crash. The skin stiffens and the fruit doesn't split or break up.

My impactful innovation has been jumped on by car engineers. They are creating new metal alloy foams based on my fruit's structure. These are lighter and cushion heavy impacts better than existing materials. One day, they may be fitted inside crash helmets, clothing and car panels, all to protect people. **Those lucky humans will stay safe with a pomelo-ing, instead of a pummelling!**

# PLANT ARCHITECTS

Architects have long been inspired by the natural world around them. Some have created bold and eye-catching building designs based on particular plants and their features.

## *Lotus flower*
## TERRIFIC TEMPLE

I'm a wetland plant whose large flowers have inspired a number of buildings. One of the grandest is the Lotus Temple in Delhi, India. Its twenty-seven walls are shaped and arranged like my petals and are covered in white marble. Surrounding the temple are nine water pools each shaped like my leaves. They create the illusion of the temple floating on water — just like I do!

## *Calla lily*
## FLOWER POWER

I'm a beautiful ornamental plant from southern Africa. My cone-shaped flowers contain a large, tall stalk called a pistil. It's where I make my seeds. My striking design has been copied by the New Energy Institute in Wuhan, China. Its outer buildings are leaf-shaped, and its inner structure is tall and white — just like my flowers. The building's roof is covered in solar panels and from it rises a yellow tower, which looks like my pistil. It doesn't make seeds, but it does produce electricity using its built-in wind turbine.

## Palm tree
# UNFINISHED BUSINESS

My stout trunk and branches may have inspired Spanish architect, Antoni Gaudí. He designed a forest of stone columns to hold up the ceiling of his amazing La Sagrada Família church. The columns are shaped like my trunk at their base and branch out at the top, just like my branches, to spread the load they support. Work on this extraordinary building in Barcelona, Spain, began in 1882 and hasn't finished yet!

## Spider lily
# TALLEST TOWER

I'm a desert plant with large lobed flowers around a central core. My flower design inspired the world's tallest building, the Burj Khalifa in Dubai. The building's three-lobed shape helps to deflect winds and stop them from causing the 828-metre-tall tower to sway. It also means more of the rooms in the gigantic 160-floor building have amazing views!

··· Tumbleweed ···
# LONG—DISTANCE TRAVELLER

**Most plants stay in one place, but I'm a wanderer.** In spring and early summer, I grow into a bush with delicate flowers and red and purple striped stems. As winter comes, the brittle bushy parts of me above ground snap off from my roots below. Cut loose from my anchor, I am then free to tumble, trundle and roll, blown by the wind. I can travel great distances to disperse my seeds... and what a lot of seeds I carry, around 200,000 per plant.

There are others that do what I do, such as pigweed and tumbling mustard, but I like to think I'm the best. I'm originally from Russia, so some people call me prickly Russian thistle, but I have spread across much of the United States. When I'm young, cattle, prairie dogs and other animals think I'm good to eat, but as I grow older, I get woody, spiny and not so tasty. In some places I'm considered a problem as my tumbling and travelling has seen me take over large areas of land.

My bad reputation may change, though, as I'm inspiring scientists to think up new ways of exploring other planets. Wheeled rovers that inch across Mars can be slow. NASA's Perseverance rover, for example, has a top speed of just 150 metres per hour. A rover-explorer that looks like me could be blown by the winds on Mars and simply roll around the planet's surface. What wandering that would be! Such a machine would travel much faster than a wheeled rover, especially as Martian winds can gust at over 100 kilometres per hour.

Several teams of space engineers are testing out designs, including Team Tumbleweed in Austria. These young scientists are building 5-metre-wide versions of me, packed full of scientific instruments. They reckon a tumbleweed rover could cover more than half of Mars' north pole region in three weeks or less. That's extreme exploration!

# ···Sycamore seeds···
# SPEEDY SEED–SPINNERS

**I'm not only pretty, I'm useful, too!**
I'm a tall deciduous tree with strong roots that anchor me in the soil. I'm sometimes planted in windy areas to act as a natural wind break. My timber is hard and strong – perfect for carving into fine furniture or wooden spoons and spatulas. Caterpillars feast on my five-lobed leaves whilst my little green flowers, which hang in spikes, are loved by bees seeking pollen and nectar.

Scientists get in a real spin about my super seeds. I produce a lot of these – as many as 10,000 each year. What's so special about them? Well, my seeds have wings!

HOW TO FLY

dance

Wind

Let's SWIRL!

LITTLE SEEDS

When a seed falls from my branches, the rushing air causes its wing to spin round like the rotor blades of a helicopter. Luckily, seeds don't get dizzy! The seed falls slowly towards the ground, much slower than if it lacked a wing. This means it spends more time in the air, giving the breeze more of a chance to blow it a long way away from me. It's important to spread my seeds over a wide area so that new young trees can grow up with more space to thrive.

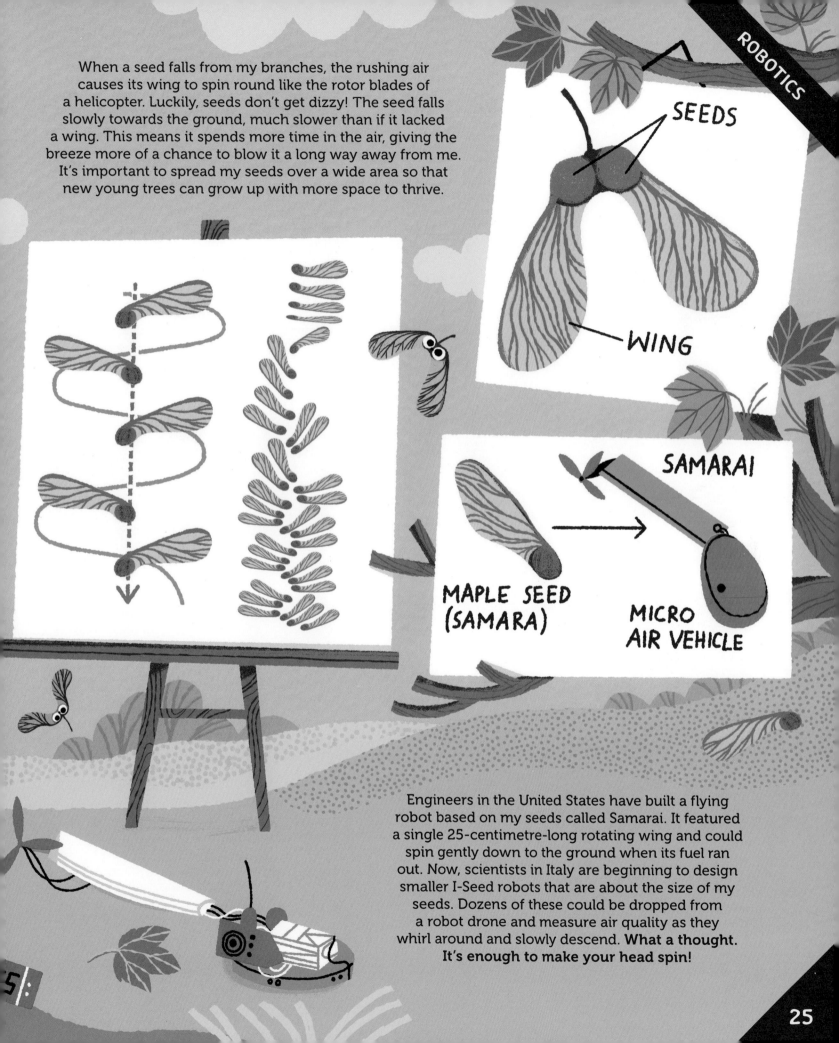

SEEDS

WING

SAMARAI

MAPLE SEED (SAMARA)

MICRO AIR VEHICLE

Engineers in the United States have built a flying robot based on my seeds called Samarai. It featured a single 25-centimetre-long rotating wing and could spin gently down to the ground when its fuel ran out. Now, scientists in Italy are beginning to design smaller I-Seed robots that are about the size of my seeds. Dozens of these could be dropped from a robot drone and measure air quality as they whirl around and slowly descend. **What a thought. It's enough to make your head spin!**

# ··· Venus flytrap ···
# SNAP-HAPPY SNACKER

There's only one thing I love more than the sun and that's a tasty insect... or spider! You see, I come from the United States where I live mostly in places where the soil is not the best. It doesn't give me all the nutrients I need. So, I top myself up now and then with an extra helping of ants, beetles, spiders and grasshoppers. Occasionally, I might scoff a baby frog or two. Yum, yum.

MENU

MENU

How do I do it? Well, I grow a number of traps on my stems. These are 2.5–5 centimetres long and made of two hinged plates. They smell of sweet fresh nectar to lure insects inside. Sneaky! The plates contain little trigger hairs called trichomes. If a number of these are touched by a creature, it's in terrible trouble...

You see, my trigger hairs are razor sharp. They take just one or two thousandths of a second to register a touch before I spring into action. The two plates of my trap snap shut like a deadly sandwich. CRUNCH! This takes just a tenth of a second. Digesting my prey, though, takes a lot longer – usually about four days.

CILIA

TRIGGER HAIRS

OUTER MARGIN

MIDRIB

The stiff hairs on the edge of my traps interlock like teeth and stop my prey from escaping.

Engineers are stunned by my speedy sensing and tremendous traps, which they reckon could give their robots amazing powers. One project in Singapore even attached one of my real life traps to a metal robot arm and used it as a gripper! Each trap only works a few times before it drops off and a new one grows. Scientists are hoping to construct their own, more permanent, versions. These could work on home robots of the future, making them able to grip delicate and odd-shaped objects with speed and ease.

I     II     III

# ···Mimosa pudica···
# THE SENSITIVE SHRUB

I hail from South and Central America, but you can now find me in lots of other places as well. I'm a creeping shrub with sharp thorns on my stems. My bright pink flowers look like delicate puffballs, but people are most fascinated by my leaves.

MIMOSA WEBWORM

SPIDER MITE

Each leaf is made up of 30–40 smaller leaflets, and when they are touched they quickly close up and fold together. Water pressure keeps them stiff. By reducing the pressure, the leaflets close and the whole leaf droops. It makes me look really shy and sad. When I was first discovered by scientists, I was nicknamed the bashful plant or the touch-me-not.

Why do I do this? Well, my leaves are a popular snack for many plant-eating creatures and I'd prefer to keep them on my stems rather than in their stomachs! By closing my leaves and going all limp, I appear smaller and unhealthy and my thorns are easier to spot. Grazing animals prefer fresh, juicy, healthy plants so look elsewhere for their lunch. Well, most do. I have a couple of fiendish foes: spider mites and mimosa webworms. They spin and wrap webbing round my leaflets to stop them folding up. They then suck out the leaflet's juices, killing them off and turning them brown. Grrrrr!

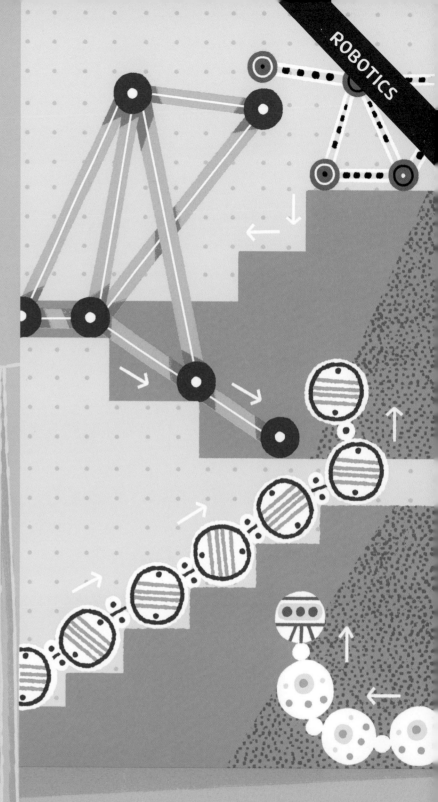

The way I use water pressure to open and close my leaves has given robotics engineers ideas. They are working on ways to control the flow of liquid inside robots to make rapidly moving robot parts that use less energy. One day, this technology might lead to robots that can change shape to perform different jobs. I think these shape-shifters would and should be called mimosa machines!

# ROBO-PLANTS

Robots are incredibly versatile machines. Many can work without human supervision for hours. Others explore dangerous places or perform dull, unpleasant jobs in factories with perfect precision and no need for toilet breaks! Robotics researchers are looking to the plant world to inspire new shapes, designs and techniques to make robots even more useful.

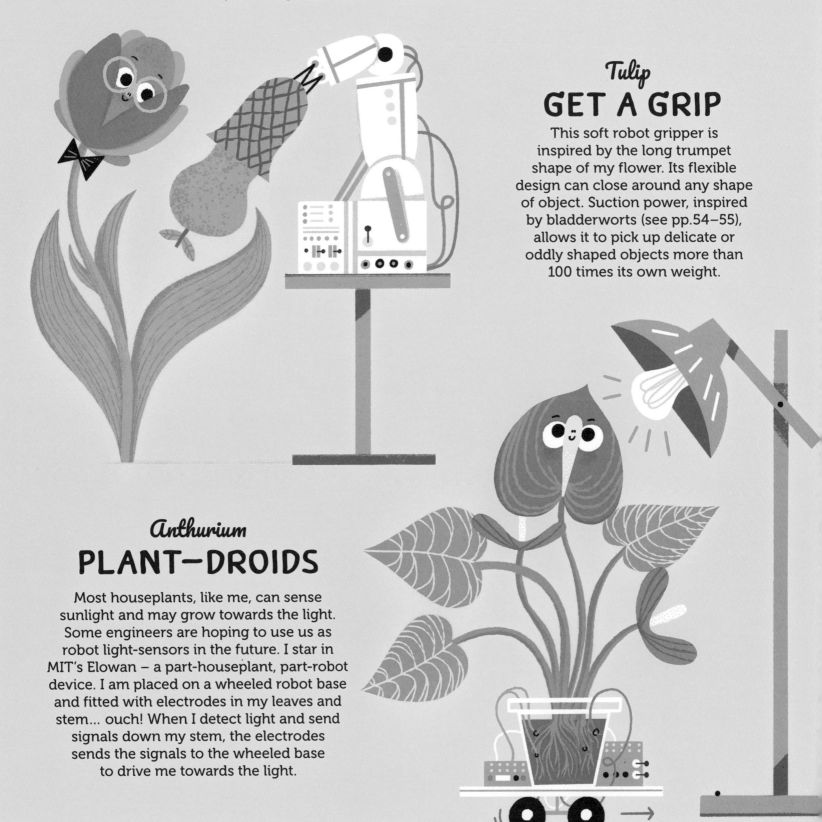

## *Tulip*
## GET A GRIP

This soft robot gripper is inspired by the long trumpet shape of my flower. Its flexible design can close around any shape of object. Suction power, inspired by bladderworts (see pp.54–55), allows it to pick up delicate or oddly shaped objects more than 100 times its own weight.

## *Anthurium*
## PLANT-DROIDS

Most houseplants, like me, can sense sunlight and may grow towards the light. Some engineers are hoping to use us as robot light-sensors in the future. I star in MIT's Elowan – a part-houseplant, part-robot device. I am placed on a wheeled robot base and fitted with electrodes in my leaves and stem... ouch! When I detect light and send signals down my stem, the electrodes sends the signals to the wheeled base to drive me towards the light.

## Vines
# VINE TIME

Vinebot is a robot inspired by how I grow. This soft, flexible tube robot, with a camera on its nose, expands in length as it squeezes through gaps and past obstacles. Future vinebots may crawl through earth or rubble to help search-and-rescue missions in disaster zones. Cool!

# ROBOTIC ROOTS

Researchers are now working on robotic roots which contain sensors. They can be 3D printed to grow longer and longer. In the future, these robot roots may spread out in the soil just like plant roots, to seek out and monitor soil pollution or even hunt out valuable minerals like gold.

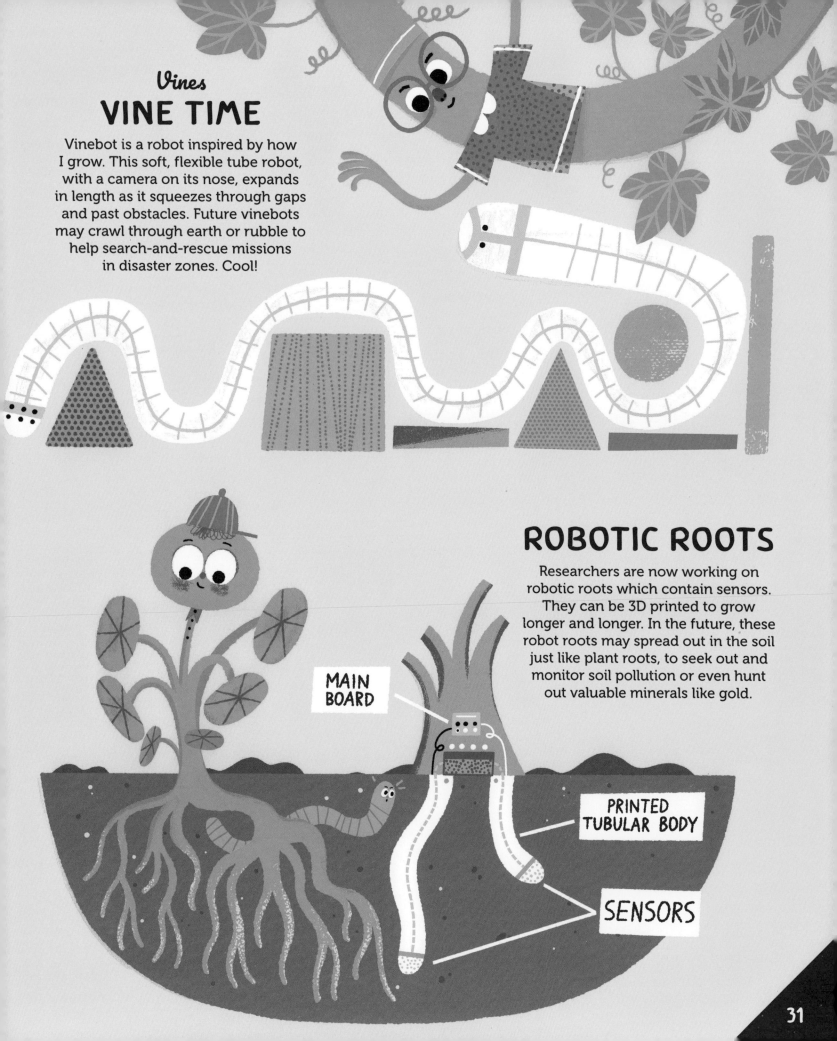

MAIN BOARD

PRINTED TUBULAR BODY

SENSORS

# ··· Kelp ···
# THE HOST WITH THE MOST

I'm a super-sized sea dweller. I can reach 30 metres tall and grow up to 50 centimetres a day. Why, in just three days, I could grow taller than you! I thrive in colder ocean waters near the coast. There, I form dense underwater forests and receive many visitors. I'm a really great host. I provide food and shelter for lots of underwater life as well as hiding places for fish being chased by their hungry predators.

Speaking of hunger, many of my visitors nibble away at me, but spiny sea urchins are the worst. They really gobble me up and would be a real threat if it weren't for my friend, the sea otter. Sea otters, you see, like nothing more than to tuck into sea urchins for supper.

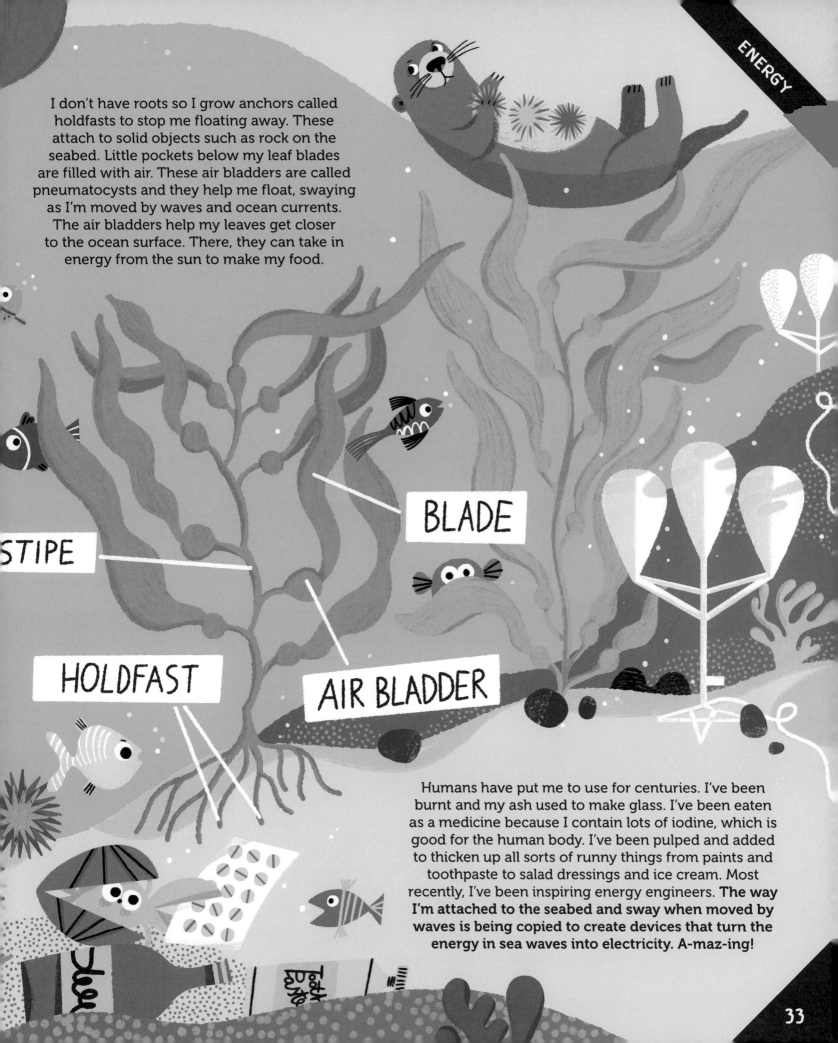

I don't have roots so I grow anchors called holdfasts to stop me floating away. These attach to solid objects such as rock on the seabed. Little pockets below my leaf blades are filled with air. These air bladders are called pneumatocysts and they help me float, swaying as I'm moved by waves and ocean currents. The air bladders help my leaves get closer to the ocean surface. There, they can take in energy from the sun to make my food.

STIPE

BLADE

HOLDFAST

AIR BLADDER

Humans have put me to use for centuries. I've been burnt and my ash used to make glass. I've been eaten as a medicine because I contain lots of iodine, which is good for the human body. I've been pulped and added to thicken up all sorts of runny things from paints and toothpaste to salad dressings and ice cream. Most recently, I've been inspiring energy engineers. **The way I'm attached to the seabed and sway when moved by waves is being copied to create devices that turn the energy in sea waves into electricity. A-maz-ing!**

··· Sugar cane ···
# FUELLING CARS AND CREATURES

As you probably know, fossil fuels like oil, gas and petrol are causing big problems. When they're burned they release greenhouse gases such as carbon dioxide into Earth's atmosphere. These cause the atmosphere to hold in more heat, which warms our planet and causes climate change. Fortunately, I'm here to help.

CAKES

SWEETS

I'm a stiff-stemmed type of grass. My stalks grow around 5 centimetres wide and up to 6 metres tall. People have been chewing on my stems to get at the sweetness inside for at least 10,000 years. In more recent times, you have all gone sugar crazy and I've become one of the world's most common crops. I've been planted all over the world, anywhere that's warm and relatively wet. Once I'm fully grown, I get crushed, heated, cooled and refined to produce the sugar you might sprinkle on your cereal or bake in a cake.

Something you should know about me is that I'm very juicy. My juice can make up as much as nine-tenths of my weight. Instead of being processed into sugar, my juice can be converted into alcohol by a process called fermentation. The alcohol made is called bioethanol and it can be burned instead of fossil fuel to produce power but with less overall greenhouse gas emissions. My stem fibres left over from making sugar are called bagasse. These can also be turned into bioethanol. Brilliant!

GREEN LEAVES

STALK

DRY LEAVES

BIOFUEL      BIOFUEL

ECO      BUS

BioFUEL

BioFUEL

CO₂

Some countries run bioethanol buses or mix a little bioethanol in with petrol used to fuel most motor vehicles. In Brazil, tens of millions of motor vehicles run solely on this fuel made from me. If less sugar and more bioethanol was produced, then I could play a bigger part in helping to tackle climate change. Wouldn't that be sweet!

35

## ··· Titan arum ···
# YOU ROTTER!

There's no two ways about it... I stink! You don't get the nickname 'corpse flower' (a corpse is a dead body) without smelling really, really bad and I absolutely PONG! Luckily, this foul odour occurs just once every few years and then only for a short time. I only smell this bad when my flowers are out and that's just for 48 hours, sometimes less.

Flies welcome!

Arum

eau de arum

Arum Amore

The thinking behind all this stinking? Well, smelling of rotting meat attracts flies and beetles who think there's food on offer. As they buzz and bustle around me, they both carry pollen from other flowers to mine and leave with my flowers' pollen on their bodies. This helps us *Titan arums* reproduce and grow new plants.

TRIPS

MAP

SOUVENI

Long queues of people gather outside botanical gardens when I'm about to bloom. It's a big event as I'm a rare plant only naturally found in the jungles of Sumatra in Indonesia. The crowds don't just flock because I'm stinky but also because I'm absolutely massive! My collection of deep red flowers grow on a giant stalk called a spadix. It grows up to three metres high – the tallest in the plant kingdom. A giant, frilly leaf, called a spathe, grows around its base.

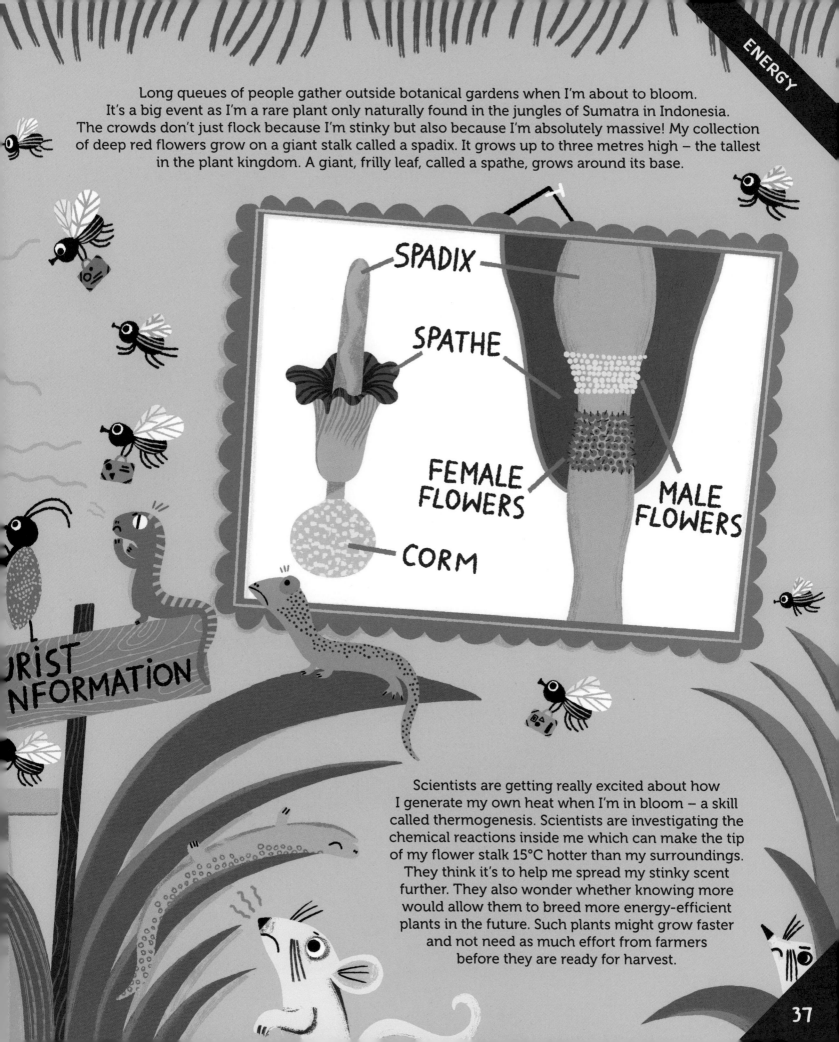

SPADIX

SPATHE

FEMALE FLOWERS

MALE FLOWERS

CORM

URIST NFORMATION

Scientists are getting really excited about how I generate my own heat when I'm in bloom – a skill called thermogenesis. Scientists are investigating the chemical reactions inside me which can make the tip of my flower stalk 15°C hotter than my surroundings. They think it's to help me spread my stinky scent further. They also wonder whether knowing more would allow them to breed more energy-efficient plants in the future. Such plants might grow faster and not need as much effort from farmers before they are ready for harvest.

··· Algae ···
# FUTURE FUEL

Move over sugar cane (pp.34-35)! We may not look like much, but algae might be the blockbusting biofuel of the future. Scientists are investigating ways to convert us into oily fuels that can be burned to create energy in place of oil and coal. If conditions are right, we can grow really quickly all year round. This means that huge amounts of us could be farmed to help meet human energy needs.

HOW TO RUN A FARM

Tiny Fellows

SEAWEED 101

SEA WEED

UNDER MICRO

Oxy

There are thousands of types of us, and we mostly live in water. Did you know that there are more of us in the oceans than there are stars in the entire Universe? Many of us are so small, such as phytoplankton, that we can only be viewed under a microscope. Some of us are much bigger, like nori and dulse seaweed, which many people eat.

Without us, Earth's atmosphere would be seriously lacking. We produce about half of all its oxygen. Life in water also depends on us as we form the start of all ocean food chains. But do you thank us for all we do? Pah! All we get are complaints about the environmental problems we sometimes cause. It's not fair.

When fertilisers and other farming chemicals are washed away by rain they can end up in rivers, lakes or oceans. These chemicals cause us to grow, fast! We form big, thick clouds that block out sunlight for plants and creatures below, some of which die.

**Farmers, stop using harmful chemicals and harvest ME to run your farms and tractors instead!**

# ··· Sunflower ···
# SUN WORSHIPPER

**Most plants like the sun. I absolutely adore it!** I grow best with at least six to eight hours of direct sunlight a day, but I thrive if there's even more. And when I say thrive, I do mean it. I often grow 2, 3 or 4 metres tall. In 2014, in Germany, I reached a height of 9.17 metres. That's a world record and as tall as some three-storey buildings.

I may have rough leaves and a rugged, hairy stem but my big, bright yellow flowers are very refined. Each 'flower' is actually made up of up to 2,000 separate flowers. My seeds develop in these central flowers. These seeds are eaten by people or pressed to make a rich oil used in cooking and soaps.

GIGANTIC SUNFLOWER

The whirling way my disc florets are arranged is called Fermat's spiral and scientists have found that it's a very efficient pattern for gathering energy. Future concentrated solar-power stations may arrange their mirrors in this pattern to capture and focus as much of the sun's energy as possible.

That's not all. As a sun worshipper, my young buds and blossoms face east at sunrise and then turn throughout the day to constantly face the sun as it travels from east to west across the sky. This amazing ability to track the sun's movement has been replicated by scientists in some new materials that can also bend and twist to point towards the sun. Scientists estimate that future solar panels covered in these could capture more than three times as much energy as today's panels, creating lots more clean, green electricity. Now, that's sunflower power!

··· Cottonwood tree ···
# WIND-POWER PLANT

Snow in June? Nope, that's just my small seeds, wrapped in fluffy fibres that look like cotton wool. I produce thousands of these inside my long clusters of flowers, called catkins. In June, these catkins burst open and fill the summer sky with a blizzard of fuzzy fibres. Because they are so light they can be carried a long distance by the wind.

I am the fastest growing of all the North American trees that lose their leaves in winter (scientists call them deciduous). I can add 2 whole metres in height a year and reach 30 metres tall. As a result of my speedy growth spurts, my wood is light and soft. People use it to make boxes and the frames of kites. So, another part of me also flies in the wind.

My broad canopy of branches can support thousands of heart-shaped leaves which jiggle about as the wind blows. Scientists have studied me and have found that a 16-kilometre-per-hour breeze rustling through my leaves creates about 80 watts of energy. They have even built a tiny version of me with thin plastic leaves shaped just like mine. The leaves hang from special plastic stalks that can produce electricity when bent back and forth by the moving leaves.

Wind power is producing clean electricity without pollution all over the world. At the moment, most wind turbines look like giant windmills or propellers. Perhaps some could look like me in the future? One day, these designs could be found in parks and open land around the world, providing power to people while also looking good. I think that would be tree-mendous!

# POLLUTION BUSTERS

Pollution in the air, water and in the ground are BIG problems but plants are here to help. Scientists are intrigued by how some plants soak up harmful substances or show us where pollution is present. Some are already being put to work.

## *Moss*
## ABSORBING STUFF

I can absorb harmful gases like carbon dioxide and sulphur dioxide as well as particles of polluted dust. Inspired by my pollution-busting properties, some cities are building walls covered in me to help clean the air. A young British student has even designed special tiles made of me and a foam to clean up air indoors. All I need is the occasional spray of water to keep me going!

GO GREEN!

POLLUTION MAKES ME ANGRY!

STOP POLLUTION IT'S THE BEST SOLUTION!

## *Rinorea niccolifera*
## HEAVY METAL HERO

I'm a small tree which was only discovered in the Philippines in 2014. I have an amazing superpower – I can soak up lots of nickel, a heavy metal that can be poisonous, from the air or ground with no ill effects to myself. There are more plants like me who can absorb other poisonous metals. Together, we could help clean up polluted land in the future.

## Peace lily
# HOME HELPER

Like my houseplant buddies, spider plants and ferns, I can help clean the air inside a building. My waxy, evergreen leaves absorb harmful substances like benzene and carbon monoxide. I've been tested by NASA – the space people – no less. I'm also pretty with white flowers and don't need much light or water, either.

## Cotoneaster
# SUPER SHRUB

I came top of my class in tests made beside busy roads packed with traffic. All those motor vehicles belch out fumes but they don't bother me. I can absorb 20 per cent more pollution than other shrubs, no problem. So, if you planted lots of roadside hedges made of me, I could really clean up.

45

# ··· Willow tree ···
# PAINKILLING PLANT

You'll recognise me from my **dramatic and drooping crown of long branches and leaves**. They form an elegant, living arch that provides homes for birds and food for deer. I'm one of the first trees to grow new leaves in spring and one of the last to lose my leaves in autumn.

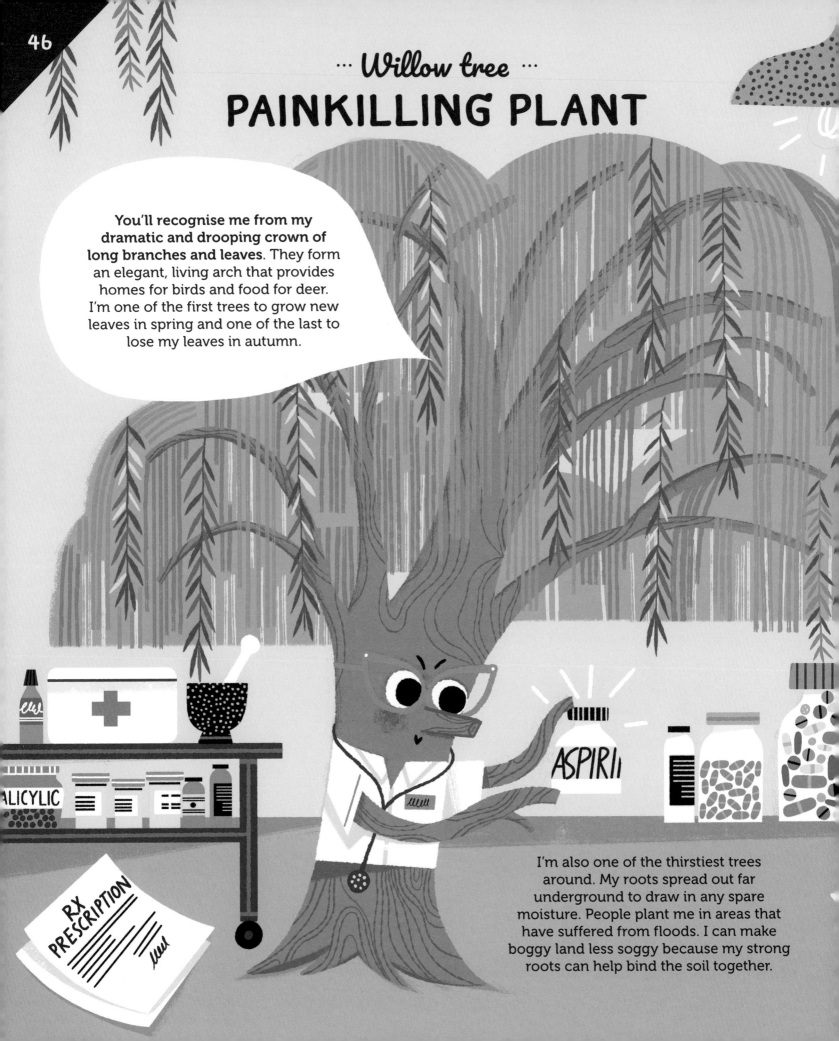

I'm also one of the thirstiest trees around. My roots spread out far underground to draw in any spare moisture. People plant me in areas that have suffered from floods. I can make boggy land less soggy because my strong roots can help bind the soil together.

The bark of my trunk has healing properties! It was chewed by ancient Egyptians with toothache and ancient Greek mums-to-be in childbirth. You see, my bark contains a powerful pain-relieving substance called salicin that works in human nerve endings. About 200 years ago, European chemists identified this painkilling chemical and started making a medicine from it called salicylic acid.

SALICYLIC ACID $C_7H_6O_3$

Aspirin

ASPIR

PAIN KILLER

Salic

Salicylic acid did a good job removing pain from muscle and joint aches. The only problems were that it tasted awful and gave many people upset stomachs. In 1897, chemists in Germany created a new version without the nasty side effects. They called it aspirin and it quickly became more famous than me! It's now the most widely taken pain relief medicine in the world. More than 100 billion tablets are swallowed every year.

··· Eucalyptus tree ···
# INSECT–REPELLING RANGER

**I'm a koala's best friend.** They like nothing more than sitting in my branches and munching on my tasty leaves. I really don't mind that much. I have thousands of them. I come in many different species, mostly found in Australia but also elsewhere. One of my trees stands an incredible 100 metres tall. That's huge.

I'm a tree of many colours. My blue-grey bark peels off in strips to reveal a yellow trunk underneath. Sometimes, a red sticky gum oozes from my trunk. My flowers are odd – they have no petals! Instead, they have dozens of little stalks which some people think look like a firework bursting. These stalks come in many bright colours from deep pink to lime green.

But that's not the only remarkable thing about me. My leaves and bark are packed with a colourless chemical called cineole. It gives me a distinctive, minty sort of smell and it's my main line of defence against hungry critters. Cineole keeps most insects and other creatures away from me. Only koalas and ringtail possums can munch on me big time and not get ill.

Scientists have found that cineole is antiseptic, meaning it can kill germs and bacteria. Cineole is extracted from me and used to disinfect and clean cuts and wounds. And there's more. Scientists are thinking of planting me to tackle mosquitoes, which can pass on malaria and other diseases to people. I'm a thirsty tree and I can drink up large stagnant water pools where mosquitoes like to breed, and my cineole also repels them! **It means I could be double trouble for those pesky pests.**

# PLANT PHARMACY

People have used the healing properties of plants for thousands of years. They learned how barks, berries, leaves or roots could help tackle different health problems and passed the knowledge on to others. Today, more than a tenth of all the most commonly used medical drugs come directly from plants.

## *Foxglove*
## BEAT BOOSTER

I'm a striking ornamental plant with columns of beautiful bell-shaped flowers. I've been a deadly killer particularly in the past when people made poisons out of me. Thankfully, I've turned over a new leaf as my leaves are used to make a drug for heart patients called digitalis, or digoxin. This slows down a patient's heartbeat but makes the heart pump with more force, pushing more blood around the body.

## *Pacific yew*
## COMBATTING CANCER

The reddish bark that covers my slow-growing trunk was examined by scientists in the 1960s and 1970s. They found that it contained a substance called paclitaxel which is now used as a successful cancer treatment for thousands of patients.

PACLI
30 MG

## Madagascar periwinkle
# LEUKAEMIA TREATER

I'm a pretty evergreen plant found on the large island of Madagascar off the coast of Africa. Scientists discovered that a drug made from my dried leaves, called vinblastine, can tackle leukaemia in children. They are trying to find ways to make this drug in labs in bigger quantities. This is because it takes about 500 kilograms of my dried leaves to make just one gram of vinblastine.

## Goji berry
# PARASITE PREDATOR

I'm an Asian plant which grows a heavy crop of rectangular red berries each year. I've been used in traditional medicine in Asia for centuries but I may be gaining a new purpose soon. A substance made from my berries appears to attack and kill off the tiny worm parasites that cause schistosomiasis – a disease that affects over 240 million people each year. Imagine stopping a deadly disease in its tracks – that would be *berry* nice.

# ··· Mangrove tree ···
# SALTY SAVIOURS

**I live on the edge – the edge of land and sea.** I'm found on the coasts of over 110 nations in thick forests which total an area larger than the nation of Greece. I am the only tree that can thrive in salt water. Some of my species draw the salt up through their stems and excrete it out of their thick, waxy leaves. Others use their roots to take in water but filter out the salt to stop it from entering in the first place.

Speaking of roots, I put mine down in mud, sand or peaty soils – I'm not picky. They grow into a dense system underwater which trap fertile soil and stop it being washed away. My roots protect coastlines from serious damage by storms and tsunamis. As a result, people in many coastal regions are planting more of me to act as a natural storm barrier. Cool. Engineers are also building storm barriers designed to look and work like my roots to protect land. Double cool!

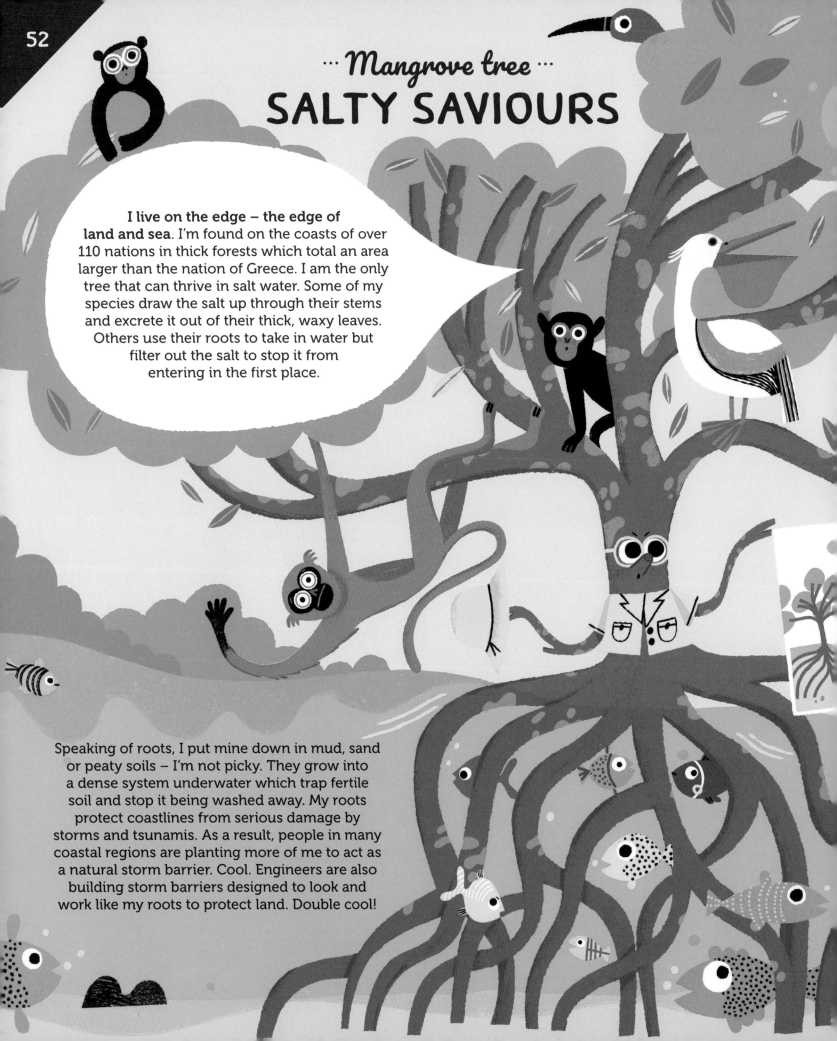

My roots, trunk and branches provide homes for creatures both above and below the water's surface. Below, many small fish, crabs and shellfish flit in between my roots. Above, monkeys, lizards, snakes and birds make homes in my branches. In some places in India and Bangladesh, the rare mangrove tiger prowls between my trunks. ROAR!

**SYNTHETIC MANGROVE**

**ARTIFICIAL MANGROVE FOREST**

**REDUCING WAVE HEIGHT BY 90%.**

Some scientists are trying to copy the ways I take the salt out of water. They are building new types of pumps so they can turn salt water from the oceans into precious freshwater, which is vital to life. **One group of scientists have even built an artificial me, packed with tiny tubes that filter the salt out. Tree-tastic!**

# ··· Bladderwort ···
# SO LONG, SUCKERS

I may look harmless, but I'm actually a speedy assassin. I'm happiest in wet surroundings such as lakes, streams and boggy, waterlogged soils. I don't lay down roots as I have quite a different way of gaining the nutrients I need to grow. You see, I am the fastest carnivorous (meat-eating) plant around. I gobble up my prey 100 times quicker than another bug-eater, the Venus flytrap (pp.26-27).

Each hollow, balloon-shaped leaf, known as a bladder, is sealed tight by an elastic trapdoor. It's covered in tiny trigger hairs. These are very sensitive. If a small creature like a water flea, baby insect or tadpole touches these hairs, the trapdoor snaps open. Because the bladder is empty inside, it acts like a powerful vacuum cleaner and sucks water and the creature inside. WHOOSH! Before it knows what's happened, the trapdoor slams shut. This all happens in one or two milliseconds – far quicker than a blink of your eye.

My killer design is being copied by American scientists to help control mosquitoes, which can spread deadly diseases like malaria. They're testing out large versions of my bladders that are powered by the sun and called UPods. These float on water just like me but trap lots of baby mosquito larvae before they can grow up into adult mosquitoes. The device sucks in the larvae along with water, kills them off, then empties quickly, ready to catch the next batch moments later.

# HOW MY BLADDERS WORK

**INSECT APPROACHES** → **SUCKED IN** → **TRAPPED**

**SOLAR PANEL**

**AIR CHAMBER HELPS UPod FLOAT**

 UPod

**TRAPDOOR OPENS, SUCKING MOSQUITO LARVAE IN**

Me? Well, I'm not solar-powered and don't work quite so quickly. After I've oozed chemicals into my bladder to digest my dinner, I'm ready to go hunting again, usually in an hour or two.

··· Acacia ···
# PEST CONTROLLER OF THE PLAINS

**I'm a large, thorny tree that provides welcome shade for birds.** Scientists are now flocking to me with a thorny problem of their own – how to find cleaner, greener ways to protect plants. You see, many farmers spray their crops with chemical pesticides to kill off plant pests. Some of these chemicals, however, can harm other living things, mount up in the soil and pollute rivers and streams.

I have a range of clever defences besides my thorns. For starters, I produce substances called tannins which make my leaves taste really disgusting. I can also talk to other trees! When I start to get eaten by a giraffe or other creature, I release ethylene gas into the air. This travels up to 45 metres away and alerts other acacia who start to produce more bitter tannins in their leaves.

Some of my species have yet another line of defence. We enslave armies of ants by providing them with sickly sweet nectar. It contains a chemical that makes it impossible for the ants to eat anything else. So, they stay on us and defend their only food source fiercely, killing off other insects and any arriving plant pests. Genius!

•ENEMY•

Scientists aren't looking to create insect armies, but they are experimenting with making plants that can alter their tannins or produce their own natural pesticides. Some modified plants are already being grown on farms, such as Bt-corn. It produces a poison that kills off certain insects that like to eat corn (pp.64-65) whilst keeping other insects like bees safe.

# PRICKLY CUSTOMERS

Cacti are some of the most fascinating plants on the planet. They can survive in the driest places on Earth by storing the little water that comes to them for a long, long time. There are more than 1,500 species of cacti. Scientists are studying some of these to find new ways of storing water, tackling pollution and making energy in sustainable ways.

## Cactus roots
## SUPER SOAKER

Many of us cacti have shallow roots that grow only a few centimetres below the surface. Our roots may not go deep but they do spread widely to seek out every drop of moisture in the ground. When it's been dry for days and weeks, the roots dry out and shrink. This creates lots of air gaps that stop water escaping from the plant back into the soil.

Now, scientists in South Korea have copied our super-duper roots. They've made a material out of gels called CRIM which can soak up water 930 times faster than it loses. CRIM could be used to store lots of water in dry farmlands, or as a super sponge in medicine or in some industries.

Desert NEWS

CRIM!

## Prickly pear cactus
# WASTE NOT, WANT NOT

I can grow up to 7 metres tall and am harvested in Mexico to be eaten in salads or turned into flour for tortillas. The waste parts of me used to be thrown away. Now, they're chopped up, mixed with cow manure (pooh!) and left to warm up and bubble away in big tanks to make biofuel. This can be used instead of oil or petrol.

PETROL OIL

BIOFUEL

## Bunny ear cactus
# SOLVING SLICKS

I'm a cactus from the Americas with no stem or leaves. Instead I grow oval pads that start out red and turn a deep green as I get older. These pads are covered with delicate cone-shaped spines which can attract water droplets from out of the air, scientists have found. Other scientists, in China, are making copies of these spines to create devices that can separate water from oil to clear up oil spills and slicks. *Oil* love to see that slick solution used to clean up the oceans!

# ···Flax···
# STICKY SOLUTION

I've been grown all over the world and clothed Kings and Queens, Emperors and Ancient Egyptian mummies. Long fibres from my stems are two or three times stronger than cotton and have been turned into linen fabric for thousands of years. I take around 100 days of growing before I am harvested and made into cloth or used as an ingredient in high-quality paper.

I reach around 1 metre tall and bloom with small blue flowers containing five petals. Occasionally, my flowers are white or pink. My seeds are now eaten as a health food or are pressed and pounded to make linseed oil, which is used to protect wood.

Speaking of wood, some of the most common building materials in the world are plywood and fibreboards. These are made of small pieces of wood bonded in layers firmly by strong glue. The glues used are created from poisonous oil – the fossil fuel used to make petrol for cars. Locked in the wood, they're safe, but when the wood rots away, the glues remain and can be harmful.

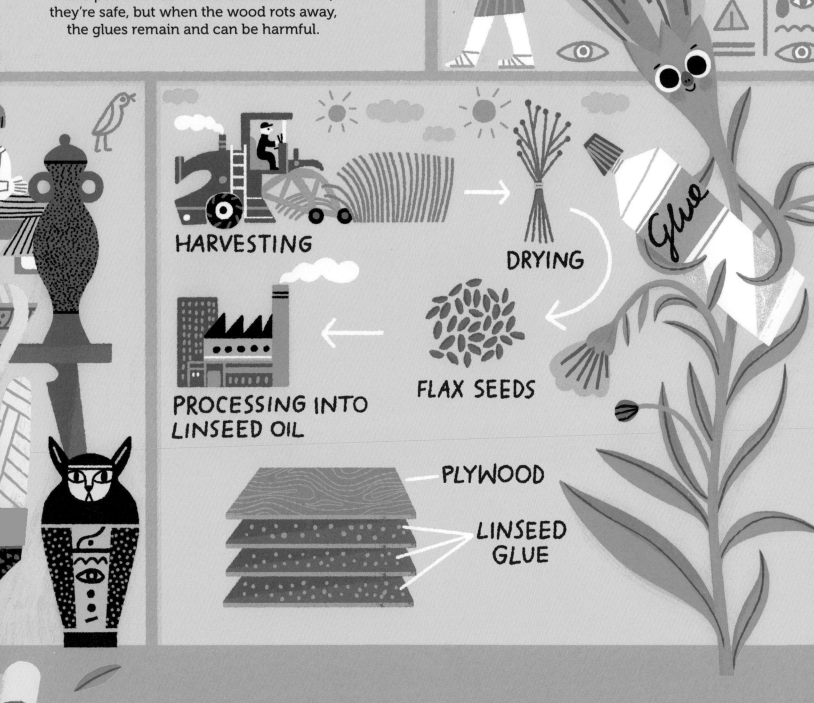

HARVESTING

DRYING

Glue

FLAX SEEDS

PROCESSING INTO LINSEED OIL

PLYWOOD

LINSEED GLUE

Chemists are on the way to solving this sticky situation by turning to nature. They are making a glue from me and my linseed oil that is not toxic and does rot away in time. The glue, which looks a lot like raw honey, takes ten minutes to set and forms a strong bond. **If all-natural glues like this can do the job, they will help make plywood and other materials easier to dispose of and recycle.**

## ··· Salvinia ···
# THE FRICTION–FREE FERN

I'm a free-floating fern and a bit of a pest. I originally come from Brazil but have since spread around the Americas. I like to hang out in slow-moving water, floating on its surface. I can multiply and grow quickly. It doesn't take me long to clog up some rivers, streams and ponds with my leaves, which form dense mats, sometimes 50 or 60 centimetres thick. These block sunlight from reaching plants in the water beneath me. They can also prove a real nuisance to boats trying to cruise along a waterway.

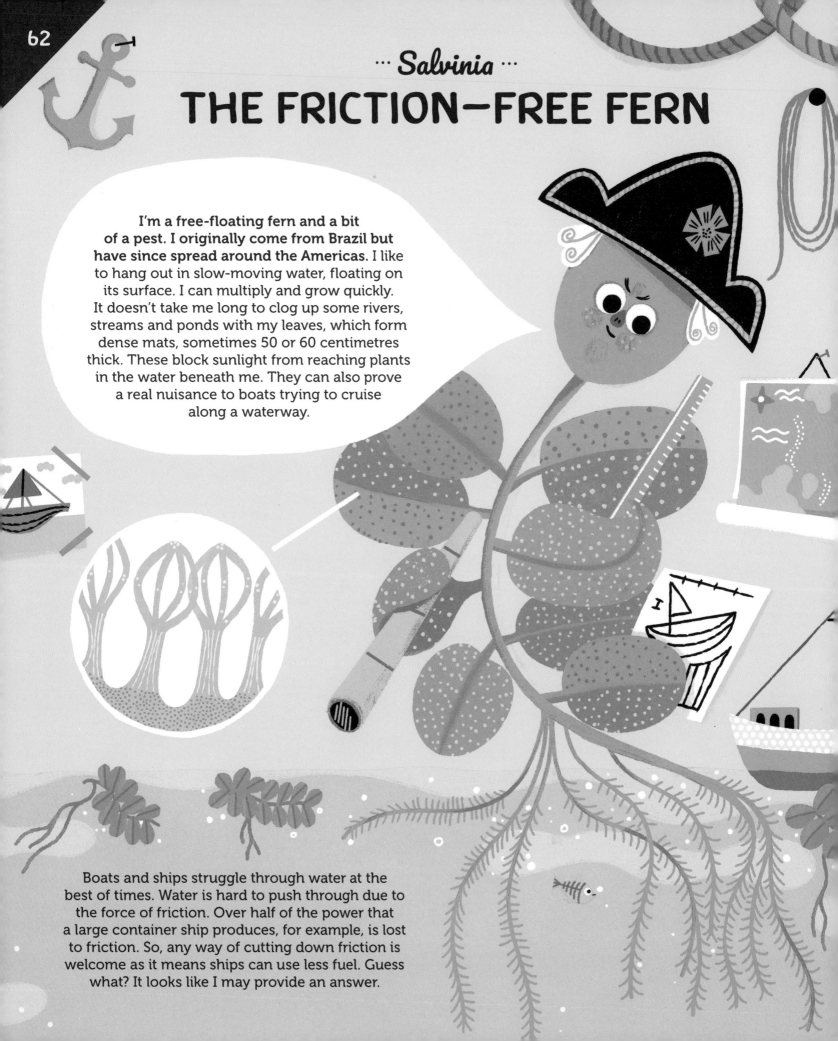

Boats and ships struggle through water at the best of times. Water is hard to push through due to the force of friction. Over half of the power that a large container ship produces, for example, is lost to friction. So, any way of cutting down friction is welcome as it means ships can use less fuel. Guess what? It looks like I may provide an answer.

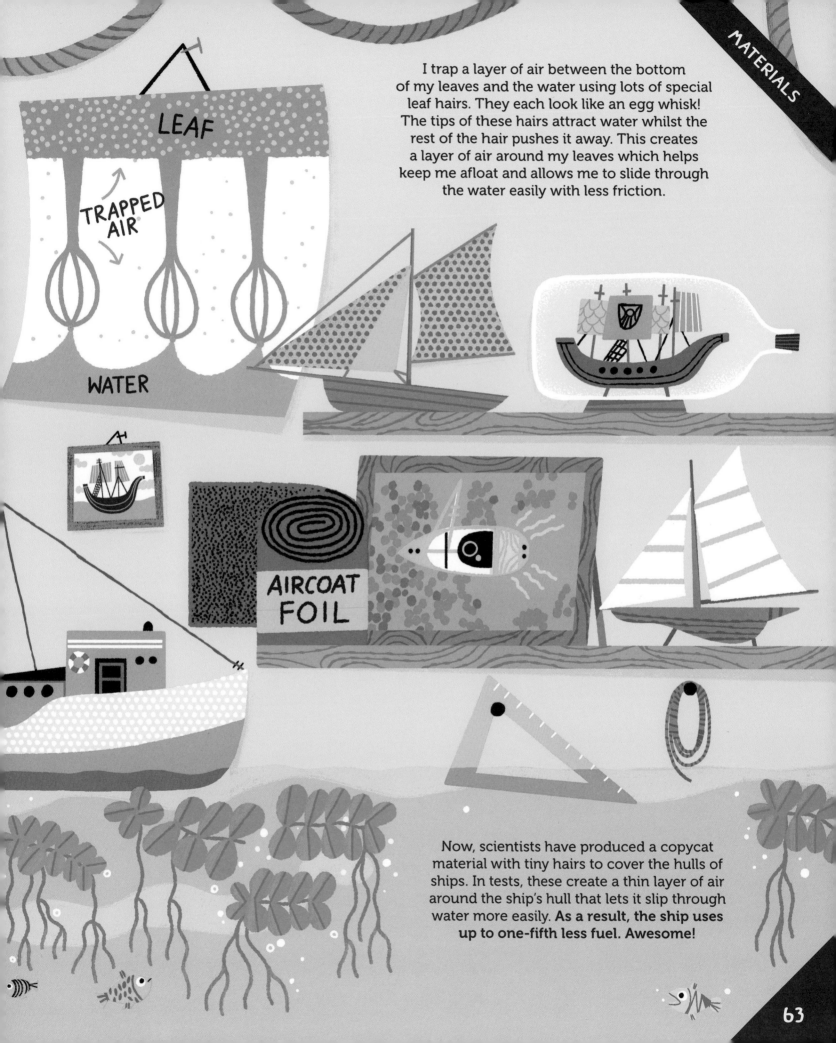

LEAF

TRAPPED AIR

WATER

I trap a layer of air between the bottom of my leaves and the water using lots of special leaf hairs. They each look like an egg whisk! The tips of these hairs attract water whilst the rest of the hair pushes it away. This creates a layer of air around my leaves which helps keep me afloat and allows me to slide through the water easily with less friction.

AIRCOAT FOIL

Now, scientists have produced a copycat material with tiny hairs to cover the hulls of ships. In tests, these create a thin layer of air around the ship's hull that lets it slip through water more easily. **As a result, the ship uses up to one-fifth less fuel. Awesome!**

··· Corn ···

# AN A—MAIZE—ING MATERIAL

I'm a tall and proud member of the grass family whose grains help feed the world. I've been grown and eaten by people in Mexico and Central America for thousands of years. When Christopher Columbus and other European explorers and colonisers found me more than 500 years ago, they took me back home. I was a smash hit with farmers in Europe, then also in Africa and Asia.

Sweet CORN

I'M NOT PLASTIC

Today, more of me is grown than rice or wheat. In fact, all the cornfields in the world take up five times as much space as the whole of the UK! Much of my crop is fed to pigs and cattle. Some of the remainder is made into breakfast cereals, tortillas and cornbread. That's just the start. I'm also turned into ethanol alcohol for fuel and sugary corn syrup for candy and other sweet things. The seed kernels of some of my plants can be heated and... POP! You have popcorn.

It may sound corny, but I reckon my best work is still to come. Scientists are developing plastic-like materials from me which can be turned into food packaging, plastic bags and disposable cups, plates and cutlery. Regular plastics are made of oil and take hundreds of years to break down into small pieces. This creates a BIG waste problem. Plastic-like materials made from me, however, can fully biodegrade and rot away just like waste food. I do have to be recycled and composted in the right conditions, though. When it's hot and humid, corn starch plastics can rot away in just three months.

CORN Flour

CORN Syrup

lf Service

·MENU·

The challenge is to make materials from me which can break down quickly in a wider range of conditions. If that's achieved, it could make me a truly a-maize-ing material!

··· *Burdock* ···
# A FINE FASTENING FRIEND

I'm a plant whose seeds like to travel. They're called burrs and are covered in dozens of little hooks that stick to the fur of animals and the clothes of people. This is how I get my seeds to disperse and grow long distances away from me – they hitch a ride!

During a walk in the woods in 1948, some of my burrs attached themselves to the woollen trousers of Swiss engineer George de Mestral and the fur of his Irish pointer dog, Milka. Intrigued by my sticky seed coverings, he took a look under a microscope and discovered all my tiny hooks which catch hold in loops of fabric and fur. This gave him a brainwave.

It took years of trials and experiments before George got his invention off the ground. It consisted of pairs of long strips of nylon material. One strip had thousands of tiny hooks, just like my burrs, and the other strip was packed full of microscopic loops. When pressed together, the hooks caught in the loops, fastening the two strips firmly. Unfastening was as simple as pulling the strips apart.

George named his new fastener Velcro and sold it as an alternative to zips, buttons and shoelaces. Astronauts made great use of Velcro both in their spacesuits and to keep notebooks, tools and other items from floating away inside their spacecraft. Within a short time, George was selling 55 million metres of Velcro a year... burr-illiant!

# ··· *Pitcher plant* ···
# SLICK SPIDER—SCOFFER

**Watch out! I'm a slick operator and a slippery fella.** I lure hapless, unsuspecting spiders, slugs and insects towards my special leaves, which have formed into a tall, tube-shaped trap. My prey buzz or crawl in greedily, hoping to gobble up my sweet-smelling and even sweeter-tasting nectar. As these creatures reach the rim of my traps, they often lose their footing and fall into my tubes. Oops!

NECTAR

Alway

There's no way back for most of them. The inside of the tube is coated with a very thin film of waxy, slippery liquid. Microscopic ridges work with the liquid to make a surface more slippery than ice. It's almost impossible for creatures to climb out. Most end up doomed in the pool of liquid at the bottom of my tube where they are digested for dinner. Mmmm.

LID
NECK
TUBULAR LEAF

MOUTH

LIP

PITCHER BODY
(FLUID-FILLED)

I am found in tropical parts of Asia and Australia where I mostly grow in soil that's really acidic. I come from a big family called Nepenthaceae. There's more than 140 of us. The biggest member of our family was named after the famous naturalist, David Attenborough. It can grow 1.5 metres tall and sometimes traps and digests mice, frogs and lizards. Wow!

TV

FLIES
BEST Movies
WORMS
·SPIDERS·
COOK BOOK

LUBRICATING FILM

REPELLED LIQUID

SLIPS MATERIAL

GRY!

PS

My super-slick insides have inspired American scientists to develop materials called SLIPS made of tiny moist fibres. SLIPS is short for slippery liquid-infused porous surfaces. These materials repel water, oil, dirt and bacteria. They may be used in the future to create super-clean syringes and other medical equipment as well as windows and glass lenses that don't mist up. If these become popular then you'll have me to thank!

# ··· Guayule ···
# RUBBER WONDER

I'm a humble-looking **desert plant.** Little would you know that I contain something of great value to humans – natural rubber.

You may have heard that people make synthetic rubber from oil, but this is usually not as strong as the natural rubber mostly found in Southeast Asian tree trunks. Truck and aircraft tyres have to contain lots of natural rubber because they support such heavy loads. My rubber is the best for this as it is particularly strong and s t r e t c h y. Take that, tropical trees! It is also allergy-free. This means it can be made into gloves and stretchy wetsuits without causing skin rashes or irritation.

I thrive in the hot sun in Mexico and the southern United States where my roots spread out deep and wide to pick up any drops of moisture in the soil. My thin grey-green leaves are covered in a white wax which helps stop them from drying out. Other trees that produce natural rubber only grow in warm, wet conditions so it means I could help produce rubber in places which couldn't before.

I also grow more quickly than tropical rubber trees. I can be harvested after two to three years. Other natural rubber trees may take three or four times as long before they produce rubber. Slowcoaches! Scientists are working on more efficient ways to separate out the rubber I contain from the rest of me. **If they succeed, you might see large guayule plantations spring up in desert areas and ride in vehicles fitted with guayule tyres in the future. Cool!**

# MEGA MATERIALS

It's already amazing what can be done with plants but there's much more to come. Scientists and engineers are pushing the boundaries of research and creating amazing new substances and materials from different plant parts like tree trunks, fruit and flowers.

## *Paperbark maple*
## ALIEN CONCRETE

I'm a tall tree found in Australia with long spiky flowers. I've invaded parts of America as an unwelcome guest but now US scientists are getting their own back. My wood is being cut into chips, soaked in chemicals and turned into a rock-hard building material called alien concrete. This material is 70 per cent lighter than regular concrete and keeps heat and sound in. One house in Florida has already been built out of chunky alien concrete tiles. Many more may follow.

## Pineapple
# LEAFY LEATHER

Spiky on top, juicy inside, my fruit is a popular dessert all over the world. People don't give much thought to my leaves, though. More than 40,000 tonnes of them are thrown away each year. That may all change with the invention of a cruelty-free leather called Piñatex. It's made from my leaf fibres mixed with a plasticky resin called PLA made from corn (pp.64-65), sugar cane (pp.34-35) or sugar beet. The material looks and feels like soft leather and has already been turned into bags, wallets and seat covers.

## Milkweed
# INCREDIBLE INSULATOR

I'm a perennial plant whose pink flowers attract many insects including colourful monarch butterflies. When it's time for my tiny seeds to leave me, they depart attached to fine white fibres, which catch the breeze with ease. Scientists have found that my silky-fine white fibres are brilliant at keeping heat in – five to six times better than wool. Future insulation in jackets and sleeping bags could be made from me. Hot stuff!

# PLANT INNOVATION LAB

Here at our innovation lab, we're always thinking, examining plants and testing out what nature does best. Who knows? One of our smart, natural designs or actions may be the next big breakthrough.

## Squirting cucumber
## SEED GUN

I squirt my seeds up to 8 metres away so they can have space to grow. Could my methods of building up pressure inside my fruit be tapped to provide sudden bursts of power for machines?

## Rice
## POWER PLANTS

Bright scientists are experimenting with generating electricity from the waterlogged fields where I am planted. As I grow, I produce more sugars than I need and release the rest into the soil. There, it breaks down and produces electrons. Could these electrons be harvested as electricity?

## Water lily
# NICE PAD

Seventy per cent of Earth's surface is covered in water. In the future, as the human population gets bigger and bigger, entire cities may have to be built on water. Could we all live on giant platforms modelled on my lily pad leaves?

## Oregano
# NATURAL FOOD PRESERVER

I'm a popular herb used on pizzas, in sauces and in lots of other dishes. It turns out I also dish up a powerful blend of substances that can battle bacteria and other things which make food go off. Could I could be a natural way of keeping food fresh?

Beef

Meat

SAUSAGES

# INDEX